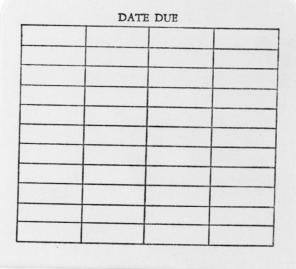

Dwellers of the Tundra

Life in an Alaskan Eskimo Village

by Aylette Jenness
with photographs by Jonathan Jenness

CROWELL-COLLIER PRESS

Library of Congress Catalog Card Number: 74-93716

The Macmillan Company
Collier-Macmillan Canada Ltd., Toronto, Ontario

Printed in the United States of America

First Printing

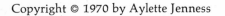

Dwellers of the Tundra

To the people of "Makumiut"
with affection and annoyance
gratitude and impatience
compassion and despair
but above all with respect

*Grateful acknowledgment is made
to the United States National Institutes of Health
for financing the research of which
this book is an offshoot.*

Contents

Dwellers of the Tundra

Introduction

■ The tundra here is a vast flat bog in summer. Inland, shallow ponds interlaced by meandering creeks spread over the land. From the air, these ponds are infinitely varied in color, ranging from dull yellow-brown through acid greens and pale blues, made more brilliant by contrast with the dark colors of the tundra growth. Near the coast, the ponds are smaller in size, more numerous, irregular in shape, until the tundra is nearly half water and the water brackish rather than fresh. Gradually the land gives way, over several miles of driftwood-scattered flood plain and a mile or so of marshy mud flats, to the cold gray Bering Sea.

A single range of hills rises abruptly from the flat land thirty miles inland and extends in a nearly straight line to the sea. Low, and rounded in gently sweeping curves on their inland edge, the hills become steadily wider, higher, steeper, until their upper slopes are barren gray boulder fields, their ridges narrow, their peaks sharp and jagged. At the sea, they end suddenly in steep, granite-spired cliffs, dropping a thousand feet to the surging water. The hillsides are cut in many places by clear, racing streams, which slow down when they reach the lowlands. Each joins the narrow river winding sluggishly along the base of the hills. The river becomes more brackish, more tidal, until at last it flows into a wide shallow bay.

■ Many of Josiah Chiftak's old tales begin,

> *There was a village,*
> *set on a hill*
> *beside a river,*
> *where the river enters the sea . . .*

And it is in just such a place that one sees, today, the faint rising smoke trails, the small cluster of rectangular shapes that mark the village. No roads lead to it, no neighbors are within a day's walk of it. It is only a tiny irregularity in this huge landscape. But to the one hundred and fifty people living there, it is the center of the world. They call it *Makumiut*, "the place of our people," for although they are Alaskans and American citizens, they are first of all Eskimos.

Within this small area, encompassing a school, a post office, two churches, two stores, a National Guard building and twenty-five houses, occurs the whole range of human feelings. The same characters appear here as may be found in almost any small American town; the rich man, the hard-luck Charlie, the browbeaten wife, the young belle. In Makumiut, though, life is more hazardous, running a little closer to the shoals of hunger, sickness, madness, accident and death.

Makumiut, "the place of our people"

part one
summer

■ But it's summer now, and summer is the easier
time, the time of abundant food, of movement out from
the village, of warmth and light. February and March
are the lean months, when even fish are thin, and sled
dogs often survive on a soup of water, needlefish and
flour. In March the sun begins to rise behind the hills;
by May its warmth has slowly melted the frozen cover
of river and stream, the thick sea ice, the layers of wind-
packed snow and finally the surface of the frost-infused
earth itself. In the long hours of light, dimmed to glowing dusk for only a short time each night, a spongy mat
of fresh green moss, grass and brightly flowering plants
springs up, covering hill and tundra with new life. The
air, which carried in winter only the rush of wind, and
the occasional croak of a raven, now rings with the
shrill piping of numberless small shorebirds and swal-
lows, the insistent calls of returning flocks of ducks
and geese, swans, cranes and loons. No longer icy cold
and pure, the breezes are rich with the smells of salt
water, mud, earth, rank plant growth.

The houses of Makumiut open up. Doors are left
open, windows unchinked and sometimes even taken
out of the walls to let in the fresh air. Babies and toddlers, who have hardly been outdoors all winter, bounce
around on the backs of older sisters, and Annie Chiftak
is given a wagon ride by her brother. Women sit outdoors, plucking the birds that daily fill each cooking
pot, while bits of feathers, summer's snowflakes, fly
about and land in their hair. Small boys, pretending
they are Superman, run about flapping the largest geese
wings they can find. Skiffs are built or repaired, out-
boards overhauled, Ephraim Aliyuk makes a new net
while his young grandson watches.

In summer, men, women and children scatter from
the village to forage on hillside and tundra, in ponds,
creeks, river and sea.

The women and girls know where and when to

collect each useful plant; the spinachlike greens called *naskobaguak*, which sprout along tundra stream banks, the juicy red and yellow sourdock, the crisp wild celeries and tender ferns unfolding by suddenly gushing hillside springs and rivulets. They gather fat salmon berries brightening the lowlands in July, and later roam the hills to pick many bucketsful of tiny black crowberries, each one only a squirt of tart juice and a crunch of seeds, but welcome indeed to people who grow no food. Again they come across the familiar graves of their ancestors, returned to the earth but for a few crumbling bones.

9 The birds are perhaps the most dramatic of summer's bounty, for the area around Makumiut is one of the great waterfowl breeding grounds of the world.

The people are far more familiar with their birds than with their plants: they have names for perhaps a third of the flowering plants in their area, but virtually all of the birds. Any grown man can identify and name a hundred different birds, from the rarely seen golden eagle to the common cackling goose. He knows their breeding, nesting and feeding habits, and where and when to expect to find each one. He hunts four different species of geese in great number, and more than a dozen kinds of ducks. Often he shoots larger shorebirds, cranes, loons or even, surreptitiously, the prohibited whistling swan.

Every male old enough to shoot spends long hours, day and night, on hillside and tundra, patiently crouching behind hillocks of grass or bush, waiting for the flocks of birds to pass overhead. Young boys run about the shallow ponds between the village and the river, trying to shoot shorebirds with slingshots or bows and arrows, and sometimes succeeding. More often they come home with a capful of tiny speckled eggs to share with their small brothers and sisters.

Egging is a favorite activity. As soon as the birds have nested, parties of girls cross the river to comb the tundra, walking slowly across the hummocky ground, noting expertly the slightly rounded grass of a shallow nest, the pale olive greens, tans, or speckled browns of the eggs against the dull moss. They return home late at night, muddy, mosquito bitten, damp from intermittent rains, but quietly laughing and talking together, well pleased with their outing, and with the store of eggs packed safely in grass baskets on their backs.

The annual goose drive brings out almost the whole village, for this is a community enterprise held each August ever since anyone can remember.

In the cool gray early morning light, half-a-dozen young men cross the river, and walk five or six miles north across the tundra, parallel to the coast. Then they head toward the sea, and turn back again, spreading out in a long line, swinging sticks and herding in front of them the flightless molting emperor geese and their young, who live along the tidal plain. In the late afternoon people stream out of their houses down the hill and pile into all available boats. They motor downriver almost to the sea and trudge out onto the tidal flats to set up a V-shaped fence of fishnet. Under the direction of a village elder, they spread out as arms of the V and crouch in the grass, the adults ineffectually shushing the excited children. Soon the figures of the young men appear across the dull green marsh. Then, as they draw nearer, a gentle rustling sound grows in the air, and soon dozens of long-necked, fat-bodied geese appear. Quietly, the people stand up and close in on them. The geese huddle together, bobbing their slender black and white necks, turning their heads from side to side and fluttering their useless wings, waddling slowly, awkwardly. The young, peeping softly, scuttle spasmodically here and there among the adults. Surprisingly docile, the geese allow themselves to be neatly separated into two groups. Immediately one group is hustled into the enclosure; a net is drawn across the open end. Several men jump inside and begin killing the geese with a quick wring of the neck, throwing each one over the net. A gosling escapes, but a watching girl chases and hits it with her stick. The pile of dead birds grows; the other group is herded in and killed. Then all are loaded into skiffs, and the people return to the village. Two of the older men divide the catch; ten adult birds and a

Young men herding the
emperor geese

pile of young for each household. It has not been a particularly good drive. Some people say there were not enough drivers, others that the line of drivers was not slanted properly and many birds must have escaped inland. One driver thinks that there should have been more villagers to meet them and funnel the geese into the net. Still, no one quarrels; there is what there is, and families happily collect their share. Many birds will be boiled and eaten tonight, others hung in entryways for the next few days. Some will be skinned and dried; the meat will be welcome when the birds have gone, and the skins, turned feather side in, make warm soft booties. Several small goslings are now pets of the youngest "hunters"—for a few days, anyway.

12

The villagers have funneled the geese into the net

*Many will be boiled
and eaten that night*

The Bering Sea brings many riches in summer, not the least of which is a vast quantity of driftwood. Far away from Makumiut, in the heavily forested interior of Alaska, trees fall from cut-banks and float as far as two thousand miles on the winding Yukon River before reaching its mouth. There the Bering Sea current picks up the timber, carrying it south and depositing thick heaps on shores and islands for more than a hundred miles. In treeless Makumiut, this wood is greatly prized. Logs of spruce, birch, poplar and aspen are towed upriver by boat and laboriously hauled into the village for building houses, sleds, fish traps, tools of all sorts, and for firewood in the winter.

By far the most important of the sea's resources are the fish. Each summer huge runs of herring and salmon crowd in from the open sea to spawn, the herring on rocky shores, the salmon far upstream in creeks and rivers. And the people of Makumiut move out to catch them, using methods as old as a simple basket trap of split driftwood, and as modern as well-hung nylon gillnets tended by power boats.

Josiah Chiftak, the oldest man in the village, sets his fish trap in the river to catch dog and humpback salmon, and a number of smaller fish. His grown son taps the herring run, going downriver by motor boat to the bay beaches the herring choose for spawning. The young man sets a fifty-foot-long gillnet among the thickly milling fish, and in the space of two days has all the herring, mixed with flounder, that his skiff can carry and all that the women of the family can split, gut and hang up to dry for use in the winter. The women go along on this trip to gather from the beaches the egg-covered seaweed which is dried, then soaked in water and eaten raw in winter, when it provides a welcome change in diet.

The herring trip is hurried, though, for most of the villagers are anxious to move to the mouths of the

15

Making a basket trap is a necessary art in Makumiut

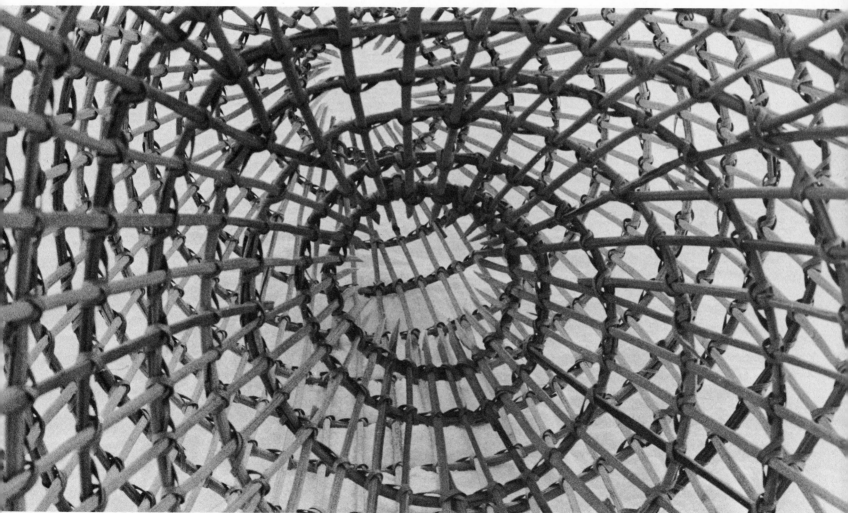

A fish trap is set in the river

Yukon River, where the salmon run in huge numbers. A commercial fishery has grown up here, and a man can earn a thousand dollars in a good five-week season. His wife may make five hundred dollars as a "slimer," cutting and cleaning the fish before they are salted, shipped to Seattle and finally sold in delicatessens as lox.

This is the major source of cash income for most of the people, so it is with a sense of anticipation that they pile tents, clothing, bedding, equipment, and even their sled dogs, into skiffs and larger boats. They travel all day and through the shimmering night along the shallow coastal waters. As important to them as the money is the fact that at fish camp people break the confines of close family living and visit with friends and relatives from other villages who have also come to fish the salmon run. Some families go to a small saltery run by a Makumiut man, others to several companies owned by white men from "Outside." Families split up, young people often living in tents with cousins or friends. In a village so small that many of the unmarried young people are each others' first cousins, the social life of fish camp, in spite of constant rain and mud and hard work, is a high point of the year.

If Makumiut can be said to have a harvest, it is a harvest of salmon. Only the largest species—the king salmon—is sold. The others—dog, humpback, silver— are eaten fresh during the season, and in such quantities that people grow tired of even that rich delicious flesh; they eat for variety the cleaned intestines, the egg sacks, the boiled bones. Even the sled dogs live on guts and eggs. The heads and backbones with adhering flesh are dried for their winter food, when they will need the energy the oily fish provides. Kegs of salted salmon are put up for the winter, and huge quantities of fish are split, smoked and dried, forming a prized Makumiut food. Rich, oily, sprinkled lightly with salt, the dried salmon is a true delicacy.

Egg-coated seaweed and the heads and backbones of salmon are dried for winter use

The villagers pack up and travel
to a commercial fishery,
where they can earn some money

*They travel through the day and night
along the shallow coastal waters*

*At fish camp people break the
confines of close family living
and visit with friends and
relatives from other villages*

This food, together with dried herring, flounder, egg sacks, egg-covered seaweed and small barrels of greens and berries, lasts well into the winter. In the old days this food meant at the least a welcome variation on the late winter diet of fresh fish, and sometimes the difference between survival and starvation, if winter fish runs were poor and seal hunting hindered by bad weather. Today there is also white man's food, and it is the arrival of this which brings the villagers hurrying home from fish camp.

Each year the *North Star*, a government freighter, brings supplies from Seattle to Alaskan coastal villages. The people of Makumiut never see it, though, for the coast is so shallow here that the ship anchors nearly seven miles out to sea, and the goods are ferried to shore in its barges.

As the time approaches for the *North Star* to arrive, the village draws together again and stirs with anticipation The tram car for hauling goods into the village must be repaired, and its battered track cleared of dirt. The winch is oiled, and the gasoline engine to power it is checked over and given a trial run.

The two storekeepers find their copies of the orders so laboriously made out last winter, so pored over, deliberated, crossed out, changed. Fruit: canned; apples, fruit cocktail, peaches, pears, pineapple, strawberries. Fruit: dried; apples, apricots, currants, mixed, prunes, raisins. Sugar: white; 1 lb. boxes, 5, 10, 25, 50 lb. sacks. Will people buy strawberries at double the price of peaches? Maybe, it's something new. Edward Chahnak has decided to chance a few cases this year. The teachers, Mr. and Mrs. Elsen, have ordered a lot for their family; the children miss the fresh strawberries of their home state, Maryland. Mike David, the young manager of the Village Cooperative Native Store, has stuck to basic staples as advised by the village council.

Salmon are split, smoked, and dried, forming a prize Makumiut food

People with cash from salmon fishing mull over possible purchases from the stores: plywood for a new floor for the house? Another glazed window? Three families have ordered snowmobiles, and the young men of these households are full of suppressed excitement; they grin whenever they meet each other.

The village buzzes with rumors. Someone says Mr. Elsen heard the *North Star* captain talking to Cook Bay on the radio a few days ago. That means Salmon Creek will follow, then Makumiut. At last the *North Star* radios Mr. Elsen; the barges will be in on the next high tide.

A young girl picking berries high on the hill is the first to spot them. Like three huge black sea creatures they appear in the bay sliding across the red and gold water of late evening. She watches a minute, then hurries down into the village. The children run from house to house spreading the news. Within a few minutes the men and older boys head to the riverbank, for all available manpower is hired to unload. The barges, old World War II landing craft, churn up the river, angle in and ram their flat prows onto the muddy shore. Amidst the clanking of chains, throbbing of engines and shouted orders, the front ends are lowered. Work begins. This noise and hurry is strange to Makumiut people, but the men respond, laughing and joking with the familiar crew members, quickly setting up the slide from barge to dry ground.

First to be unloaded are the fuel drums—several hundred of them. Fuel for heating the school, the teachers' house, the stores, the National Guard building, and for the handful of people who can afford oil stoves in their houses. Fuel for the school's electric generator, and for

The barges appear in the bay,
sliding across the water

the two smaller ones, owned by local entrepreneurs who sell electricity in the winter; two light bulbs to a house, burned from the time it gets dark to ten or eleven P.M. Fuel for the gasoline lamps of those who cannot afford the five dollar monthly electric bills. Fuel for boats in summer, for snowmobiles in winter.

Next are the school supplies; all the food for the hot lunch program—dried beans, rice, canned fruit, meat, soup, vegetables, powdered milk—then the crates of books and papers, pencils and art materials, even a huge new fuel tank.

The next barge load brings rough slatted wooden crates. A large gleaming white sink can be seen inside each one; twenty-six in all. The men puzzle over this as they unload. They remember that some Gussuks—white men—flew in to the village last winter—from the Bureau of Indian Affairs, or United States Public Health Service, or State of Alaska, or maybe it was one from each. The Gussuks called a village meeting to ask if the people would like running water in their houses. The government would supply plans, pipes, sinks and materials for drainage boxes. The people were to do the work. The people agreed, though the village council chief said privately that he'd believe it when he saw it. The Gussuks flew away again. Then a letter arrived saying it had been found that the plan was not feasible, but that a large water storage tank would be sent in and centrally placed in the village. "Running people instead of running water," was Mr. Elsen's wry comment. The postmaster, Tom Apureen, wondered how the storage tank could be more centrally located than the clear, always-flowing stream along which the village had been built in the first place.

But now, here are the sinks after all—and neither pipes nor storage tank are in sight. Ah, well, probably someone will come and explain it; meanwhile, the girls

and young women have come down and are peeking excitedly into the crates which join the growing pile.

In the fall most people will install their sinks in wooden frames, with plugs where the faucets should go, and buckets where the pipes should go. The large sinks will take up a great deal of room in the houses, but most people will like them; one family will cover theirs with wrapping paper at Christmas and stand a small aluminum Christmas tree in the center.

The barges come in on each high tide; the stack of goods grows taller and taller on the shore. At the end, the village children are given a ride around the river mouth in the last empty barge, before it disappears out to sea to its unseen ship for another year.

Now the hardest work begins. The winch by the school creaks all days and half the bright night as each tram load is hauled up into the village. The children stand clear of the singing cable, watching enviously as the older boys sway and bounce downhill in the empty car.

In the stores, Mike David and Edward Chahnak try to check the goods off their lists, unpack the cases and stock shelves amid the clusters of onlookers and customers. At fifteen cents apiece, tart apples and sweet California oranges sell out within a few days; every child in the village gets at least one to savor. Teen-agers sit on the counters drinking canned sodas as long as they last. Babies and small children gaze round-eyed at plastic rattles and toys, as their mothers finger the bolts of flowered cottons, the trays of silk scarves and wool gloves. Men lounge quietly in the corners, looking at fishnets, ammunition, gear for dog harnesses. Flour, sugar, tea, coffee, even cake mixes, all sell readily. The canned strawberries, a row of brilliant scarlet labels, sit in state on a high shelf of Edward Chahnak's store waiting for the winter, when families are "just hungry" for fruit.

The hunting of sea mammals at the end of summer marks the return to a more traditional activity. Only the spotted seal, *esoyik*, hauls up on the sand islands in the bay throughout the whole summer. Men go there by skiff to wait patiently; immobile, silent, watching for the small bobbing heads to come within rifle range. A man must not only be a good shot to hit that will-o'-the-wisp target, but he must reach the carcass quickly by skiff lest it sink, for in summer the seals have only a small layer of fat beneath the skin and are not buoyant.

In September the other seals, the larger bearded seal, called *mukluk*, and the smaller ringed seal, *nyik*, as well as the white whale, come in from the sea, running along the bay shores and into the river.

The taking of a white whale is rare enough to be an exciting occasion. People come running down the hill, and men and boys strain together to haul the whale up on the muddy shore. The children stroke its sides, pure white, cool and smooth as polished ivory; they are longing to chew on a piece of the fresh, mild-tasting rubbery skin, as they did when the last whale, a baby, was caught. But they will wait until it is offered.

The older men gather and quietly debate the butchering. This whale was first shot by a young man who had never hit a whale before. Even though it was shot again, and harpooned by others, it is considered his primarily. By custom, most of the meat will be distributed around the village in his name. When the first cuts are made,

handholds are slit for the helpers, and the thick layer of fat is slowly peeled back.

Basinful after basinful of the rich dark meat and of internal organs—liver, heart, intestines—are carried up the hill as the men work skilfully and as neatly as possible on the muddy ground. The afternoon wears on, and at last nothing is left but the backbone.

Everyone will eat boiled whale tonight and tomorrow. The surplus will be cooked and stored with oil, where it will keep well enough to be used as dog food for a long time to come.

41 Summer is almost over now. It seems such a short time for all the plants to spring up, willows to sprout new growth, flowers to bloom, berries to ripen. The tender greens of early summer are now tough and stringy, the delicate ferns wither in the chilly nights. Light frosts wrinkle the berries, and people spend all the time they can gathering the last bucketsful. The tundra turns from rich green to golden yellow—pale with icy dew in the mornings, darkening to brown gold in the low rays of afternoon sun. The long chilling fall rains begin, and the land is somber under leaden skies. Flocks of ducks and geese pass overhead every day, hurrying south, calling the young to fly with them.

Soon the temperature drops, and the land begins to harden. Hummocks of grass become jagged, frost encrusted, the uneven ground beneath rock hard and rough. The resilient bounce of summer's moss is gone; the early snows merely dust the uneven surface. The tundra ponds freeze over, with a layer of ice so smooth and clear that children slide across it on their boots, watching the tiny fish scatter over the bottom.

The women of Makumiut move out to forage for the last time this year. They gather many armloads of the fine long grass which, nourished by human and animal wastes, grows only about the village. Before the snow covers it, each household must have a full winter supply to twist, as needed, into thick boot pads for insulation against the cold. Old women trudge out across the tundra, poking sticks into likely looking holes to find mouse caches of tiny roots laid up for the winter. They are guided, perhaps, by memories of the days when no bread or any other starchy food was available; in any case, everyone still likes a taste of the brown crunchy roots of sedge, cotton grass and horsetail. All women, young and old, pick sacks of *taiyaruk* to boil with fish or meat soup. Marking the end of summer, this plant is gathered only when brown and frost-killed.

part two
winter

■ In October the contours of the hill are still outlined by a rich design of brown willow and alder bushes. The river is a band of flat gray twisting across the white tundra; the sea marks its part of the horizon with a fine dark line. As the river and the sea begin to freeze over, and the snow deepens, these patterns disappear, until often only the finest differences in shades of pale gray mark where the earth stops and the sky begins.

The snow-covered arctic has an extraordinary variety for the eye, subtle, delicate, yet strong. The rich blues, purples and magentas of a clear starry dawn may be replaced by dull heavy overcast gray at noon, and then in a few minutes by blinding white-out, where all sense of distance is lost. A bush may be six feet tall and a good walk away, or tiny and almost within arm's reach. The shapes of houses, sleds, woodpiles, become

45 flat abstract patterns floating in shimmering white. And if this condition is succeeded by a heavy snow fog, then all is gone, and a person may become dizzy and disoriented walking on a level path.

Shifting, swirling, forming new drifts with each storm, day by day the snow envelops the houses, until, sometimes, the people must dig out their windows to let a little light through the frosted glass.

Now the people fall into vastly different ways of living from the scattered patterns of summer. Children are at school, nine to three, Monday through Friday, alternating between the small known world of their village and the wide world of Gussuk ideas, history, inventions, customs. Men go out by dogsled and snowmobile each day to forage, returning to the village before darkness quickly closes in. And the women?

Four Walls

■ For women the world contracts more and more as the snow deepens, as the darkness closes in, as the temperature drops. Everyone spends more time in the houses now, but for the women, all work is indoor work. And there are such great contrasts between the outdoors and the indoors. The white, windy, snow-blown open hillside may be a hundred degrees colder than the small, crowded, dim, half-buried wood house. While a man is often quite solitary outdoors, on the hills or tundra, seeing no one all day, his wife at home is rarely by herself. Probably half the women in the village are *never* alone in a house, for one minute, day or night, from October to May. And space. Few things in this world seem so enormous as the tundra, stretching out in front of the hills, seemingly without end, forever. A man scratches a minute track across this, covers in a day's work an infinitesimal part of it. But a house, a house is one or two rooms, small, too low for a woman to stand upright at the eaves, and it is her world. Everything that she sees is an intimate part of her life—children to care for, stove to tend, floor to wash, clothes to mend, water pail to fill, slop can to empty. By custom, any catch brought into the house immediately becomes hers. Outdoors, her husband may share some fish with his neighbors, but if he brings the sack across the doorway, only she can give any away.

The house is calm or tense, disordered or neat, clean or dirty, gay or morose, according to the temperament of that woman.

■ For Margaret Atootuk, her house becomes almost her entire world in winter.

She walks about fifty yards to the Catholic church for an hour each Sunday, goes to an occasional movie in the armory (but not often; she says it's too hot and there are too many people there) and attends a village meeting in the school once or twice a winter. The one house she visits is her sister's, and that only briefly a couple of times a week. She never goes to the post office when the mail plane comes in or to the store just across the path from her house. Perhaps twenty-three of the twenty-four hours she spends in a space fifteen by twenty-five feet.

Some women mind the winter enclosure; they speak wistfully of the days when they were young girls, or newly married and free of baby-tending and endless chores. Some break out of the routine by frequent visiting of neighbors. But Margaret Atootuk seems quite content, her world apparently full and satisfying.

Certainly, life is pleasanter for her now than when she was younger. There were too many little girls then, and no boys to help the father hunt and fish. The school was not built, medical help was negligible, welfare checks nonexistent. Several of her babies died —two of them longed-for sons.

Now, she has ten healthy children—from twenty-five years to fifteen months. The preponderance of girls has turned to her advantage. One daughter earns money baby-sitting for the teachers' children, one by cooking the school lunch and one receives an allowance from her husband in the army.

The Atootuk house is neat and clean. The floor shines softly, its pale spruce boards worn from countless scouring into gentle ripples like sand on a beach. The air is warm and smells strongly of soap, for today is Saturday, bath day. Early this morning the girls chopped quantities of wood and fired up the stove. They made many trips to the stream, stepping carefully down the ice ledges to the open hole, dipping their buckets into the black-looking swift current, and hurrying back to the house with fresh ice already clinking on the surface of the water. When enough water was hot, the big metal washtub was hauled out from under Margaret's bed, and each member of the family in turn soaped, scrubbed, shampooed and dressed in freshly ironed clothes. Now the older girls go unhurriedly about their jobs, sewing, sweeping, washing dishes, rolling their hair up in plastic curlers. The younger ones play house quietly, while Margaret sits in her accustomed corner of the room holding the baby—a son at last.

A neighbor brings in the latest news, staying to visit a while. Someone puts a record on the battery phonograph, while the Sears catalog is hauled out for another discussion of yard goods for making new Christmas clothes. One of the girls decides to go across to Edward Chahnak's store and buy a can of peaches for a treat, promising to bring back some bubbly gum for the little ones.

Soon it will be time to light the lamp, heat a pot of water on the stove, and pluck the white-feathered ptarmigan for supper. Father will be home from needle-fishing, night will close in. Another day passes.

■ Grandmother Chahnak was born seventy years ago in a small, partly subterranean house near Makumiut. An account by Edward W. Nelson, one of the few white men to explore the region, describes a visit to the settlement in 1878:

> . . . In the evening we arrived at a miserable Eskimo village called Igragamiut in the midst of a terrific storm of wind and snow. . . . We found our quarters in an earth-covered hut, less than four feet high in the centre, and sloping on every side. The floor was covered with a deep layer of garbage, giving rise to a horrible stench, while about the low platforms on the sides crouched a number of pasty-faced children and sickly looking elders; a litter of puppies were snuffing about among the wooden dishes in the farther end of the place. A large cake of ice served as window in the roof, and everything bespoke the most abject filth and poverty.
>
> We arose early to escape the stifling odours of our sleeping-place. . . .

Grandmother survived in this poorest of all Eskimo-inhabited areas; today she is seldom cold or wet, never ragged and, most important to her, never hungry. She is still strong and active, still sews some of the finest boots and parkas in the village. She is seldom ill. Last winter she had an infection, which she reported to Mr. Elsen at the village clinic. When medicine prescribed via short-wave radio by the doctor was ineffec-

51

tual, she was sent on the weekly mail plane to the hospital, a hundred and fifty miles away. Two weeks later she returned, cured, smiling as impassively as ever. How she felt about life in the hospital she never told anyone, but she did say the food there was pretty bad.

Her only son, Edward, with whom she lives, is a highly successful hunter, a canny entrepreneur and by far the richest man in the village. He trapped several thousand dollars' worth of mink one year, then built and stocked the first general store. The Chahnaks have the largest food storage, or cache, house in the village. Sheathed in corrugated aluminum, it is ten feet high at the ridge and grander than some homes. Inside, it is dark, strong-smelling and crammed with bundles of oily smoked salmon, strings of dried herring and seal meat, sacks of frozen tom cods and white fish. Kegs of salted salmon and seal oil and berries are stored here, as are salmon backbones and needlefish for the sled dogs. There are even sacks of seal and muskrat skins for clothing. During summer cleaning, Grandmother found a family of mice living here; surely the best-fed mice in Makumiut.

Faith Chahnak, Grandmother's daughter-in-law, has aspirations for, someday, a house with everything inside, meaning piped-in water and a toilet; but the old lady is quite content to have a well-lit place to sew beside the oil-burning stove by day, and at night, a warm bed, down-quilted, in a snug, dry house. She is indifferent to the disordered bedding, the littered floor.

It is somewhat puzzling that Faith keeps such an untidy house, for she was orphaned as a little girl and brought up by nuns at the Catholic mission a hundred miles away. There she learned to clean and launder, sew and mend, as well as to speak, read and write English. She manages to keep books for the store and deals as best she can with government forms, merchandise orders and bills. She trusts no bank, relying instead on the juggling of money orders, incoming checks and cash—any sudden need for the last always causing a scramble under beds and in corners for the battered suitcase stuffed with old clothes and money.

Faith is not a strong person. She has been hospitalized for tuberculosis, as have many villagers, and she is thin and pale. At times of stress, she talks of the worm which she says lives inside her head, crawling back and forth behind her forehead. She has had one miscarriage, no live births. She adopted a number of babies, but only two survived; an intelligent, perceptive, strong-willed and moody girl of whom Faith is very proud and a much-loved year-old boy. As an orphan and an outsider, Faith has no blood relatives for support in time of trouble. And the greatest of her troubles is her husband's drinking.

For Edward Chahnak is a rich man in a traditionally sharing society that does not like rich men. He is a man freed from the necessity of grappling each day for subsistence, in a world where this is quite new. And so, several times a year, he goes on a drunk. He starts on homebrew, holding open-house in the store from morning until midnight. He keeps the phonograph going full blast, treats the children to candy, flirts with the young girls, dandles his baby, smiles benignly on all. Then the whiskey arrives on the mail plane, air freight from Anchorage, and he grows silent, sullen, touchy with his family. The store becomes deserted, and Faith, slightly drunk too, dishevelled, wistful, starts doing all his chores. Ridden by who knows what misery, Edward tries to beat her at least once during a bout, but quickly repents, for theirs is an unusually close and interdependent marriage. He continues drinking until he collapses, ill, hungry, too weak to do anything but drink, and finally too weak even to drink.

And Grandmother? Grandmother endures, just as she has for seventy years.

■ The next house down the hill is Emily Apureen's. At fifty-two, she has twelve living children and sixteen grandchildren. The number of grandchildren will probably double in ten years; as her sister-in-law says poignantly, "The babies don't die any more."

Ten of Emily's children are living at home; a snug, tidy two-room log cabin. At almost any hour on a winter day, she can be found sitting on the floor between the window and the stove, sewing, endlessly sewing. She must keep thirteen people in boots, and each person has several pairs—patched, resoled, or new—for different purposes. The men and boys need oiled hairless waterproof ones for wet weather, and warm thigh-high sealskin winter ones. Everyone wears low sealskin boots indoors and around the village, and for Christmas each member of the family sports handsomely decorated calfskin ones. Then come the parkas —muskrat, rabbit, swanskin or quilted down. Each person must have at least one in good condition, and the young people want jackets besides—fur-outside, zippered, calfskin trimmed, with bushy ruffs of wolf and wolverine.

The Apureens have less cash than many families, and more problems. Some years ago, a married daughter was brought home from another village after trouble with her husband. Sometimes she doesn't leave the house for weeks, sometimes doesn't even come in the front room if a visitor drops by. She is pretty, frail and troubled, strong only in the watchful care and protection she gives her little boy.

The Apureens are a somber family. At home each member seems enclosed, cut off from the others. They speak seldom and in low tones. This serves to provide a great degree of privacy in a situation where no one is ever physically alone. It is, in some ways, an extension of behavior generally approved in Makumiut. One should be reserved and quiet, one should show neither anger nor curiosity. But the undercurrent of affection and humor so strong with the Atootuks is only dimly felt in the Apureen house.

Emily's oldest daughter lives next door. She is twenty-nine now and has six children of her own. Like her mother, she is an efficient housekeeper; her two rooms are amazingly clean at any hour of the day, her children are scrubbed, mended, neatly dressed. Like her mother, too, she is a little cold, impersonal. She has a sudden, almost rude, laugh which grates on the ear; it is not quite right.

Emily's second daughter, Matilda, was given as an infant to Grandmother Chahnak. She is twenty-seven now, and has had five children; thanks to the government health service, they are all alive, even the little twins. Like Grandmother Chahnak, she has a gentle exterior, reserved but warm. Like Grandmother Chahnak, too, she is a haphazard housekeeper.

■ One enters Matilda's house through a large dark entry room, which smells of fish, of seal oil and, overwhelmingly, of urine. This smell of urine—acid, sour, stale—permeates the whole household, from the baby in his sodden diapers to two-year-old Jeanie in a crusty cotton dress; from the pile of laundry soaking in a bucket beside the stove, to the stained mattresses in the airless back room.

Matilda spends most of her time in these rooms, moving heavily, slowly, from one chore to another, going outside only to bring fresh water from the stream or to empty a bucket of slops, never quite catching up with her work, never really finishing anything.

When the children are asleep at night, she tries to find time to work on the new rabbit jacket she is making her husband for Christmas. It is to be short, with the black fur outside, and trimmed at the hips with an intricate border of black and white calfskin. It will be stylish, for Will is a handsome young man, still trim and lithe. Each year she has made him the necessary long, fur-inside parka, but she has not had time to sew another jacket since the year they were married.

He wore the first one hunting muskrats that spring, and Matilda went with him. She had her own gun, a Winchester .22, which Edward Chahnak had given her.

Together they walked the melting creek banks, squinting in the light of the newly returned sun, watching for the quick brown animals. It was a good year for muskrats. Matilda traded in her skins at Edward's store and bought a set of china dishes, gold banded, which had been displayed on a high shelf all winter.

Next spring Matilda had her first baby. She left him once with Grandmother Chahnak to go hunting, but her breasts ached with the milk after a few hours, and Grandmother said he cried too much. By the following spring she was heavily pregnant again and did not try to go. She has not been hunting since.

She is not a very skilful sewer, and is worried that she has not cut Will's jacket sleeves wide enough. She hasn't. On the day after Christmas both elbows will split as he lifts an armload of firewood. He will wear the jacket with its torn flaps for another week, until Matilda can find time to cut a new piece and fit it in properly with Grandmother's help.

■ Emma Fisher, who lives nearby, has children old enough to help with all the chores, and this makes life considerably easier. The Fishers are pleased with their house, for Matthew Fisher has recently finished building an addition to its one room, removing the wall between on completion. Double its original size, it is now about twelve by twenty-five feet. The stove is to one side of the door, its string of drying clothes overhead, bucket of seal oil behind, pile of stacked firewood in a box. To the other side is a gleaming new aluminum and Formica table, with four chairs upholstered in "Starburst" pattern plastic. Emma is very proud of this table. She spent many evenings looking through the Sears catalog and finally chose the model when Matthew had sold enough mink and otter skins for them to buy it. It doesn't matter that there are four chairs and seven members of the family. It seldom happens that everyone eats at the same time, and the little ones double up anyway.

Next come the beds. First the metal-springed cot that fourteen-year-old Grace shares with little Sally. Grace complains, laughing wryly, that Sally still wets the bed occasionally; then Sally's face wrinkles, her lip trembles, and Grace must hug her, saying, "Sally, don't cry, it's OK. You keep me just warm and nice. You keep me from being scared of *ghostuks*." Across the room is the wider bed of Emma and Matthew. The boys' cots are along the back. Andrew, at twelve, has one to himself; nine-year-old Harry shares his with young Matt. Above the beds hang rows of jackets, boots, caps, mittens, parkas.

Two months ago Emma had a baby. When she started labor she sent the children to her sister's house. Then she called for her aunt, the best midwife in the village, and for the "baby box" from the clinic, with its paper sheets and pads and medicines. It was a quick and easy delivery. By evening the children were back home, and in a few days Emma was up and cooking again. Now she is feeling fine and doing all her usual work with her usual ease. But what about the baby?

■Across the village from Emma's house, past the Catholic church and beyond the Native Store stands a new plywood house. It is tall, the full height of the eight-foot plywood sheets at the eaves, even higher at the peak. Almost square, it has one door at the end away from the storm winds and a glazed window in the middle of each side. Indoors it is chilly, for a house so high is difficult to heat. There is a smell in the air of fresh pinewood, putty, new paint. A half-built cupboard crowds one corner of the room; tools and a pile of sawdust are around it. Along one wall is an old sofa, upholstered in faded maroon plush, sagging in the middle, but a Gussuk sofa nevertheless. Across from it is a new table with two chairs and on the table a folded copy of the Anchorage newspaper. The back part of the room is curtained off with long pieces of flowered cloth. On a single bed behind the curtains sits Ruby Jim, Emma's sister-in-law, looking a little stiff, a little awkward, smiling faintly. She is holding a baby in one arm, and in her other hand, a pink plastic bottle of warm milk. The only sounds are the crackle of the fire, the slightly uneven sucking of the baby and the wind which blows about the village all the time.

The morning Emma's baby was born, her mother-in-law wrapped it snugly in blankets and hurried across the village to Ruby's house, for it had been decided months ago that Emma, with five children of her own, would give this baby to childless Ruby. And the old lady was taking no chances on a change of heart.

A week later people said that Emma wanted the baby back. She hinted as much, complained a bit, moped. Her mother-in-law was on her guard, for she knew that while Matthew wanted the child given to his sister Ruby, it is Emma who makes many decisions in that household. The old lady visited Emma, brought her food, sewed a new dress for little Sally.

The rest of the village waited. It would be bad to ask for the baby back, it might cause an argument, and that would be very embarrassing. Still, it had been known to happen. Only a couple of years ago, Charley Henry got angry with his parents-in-law and took back the child he had given them, even though his wife didn't ask for it. The people wondered, the young women gossiped a little.

But now it seems almost forgotten. A few weeks ago Sally and Matt caught measles, which frightened Emma —Makumiut children often used to die of measles. Mr. Elsen came down the hill to give them medicine many times; they were very sick. Then when they got better, the bounty arrived from the Fish and Game Department for the seal faces Matthew had turned in. Emma and her oldest girl bought a calfskin from the Native Store with the bounty money, and have started to make the family's Christmas boots. Only occasionally now does Emma stop while she is sewing and look idly out of the window.

Ruby, across the village, will stay out of Emma's way for a while longer. Anyway, she is busy with her husband, her new house, her new baby; she is complete now. She has named the baby Darleen, after Mrs. Elsen, whom she likes. Besides, she thinks it is a pretty name. Father Flannery, who came to the village last month, christened her, adding Mary; Mary Darleen Jim.

■ Like everyone in Makumiut, Darleen has an Eskimo name too. There was never any difficulty in choosing it, for the Tulik baby had died the week before. No matter what Father Flannery says, everyone in the village knows that the name of one who dies should be passed on to the next one born; the old people say a spirit passes on as well.

The Tuliks were newcomers to Makumiut. They came from Salmon Creek hoping for a new start with help from their Makumiut relatives. As luck would have it, though, their skiff broke up at a rocky point on the trip, and although they and their two children were picked up, the outboard and most of their belongings were lost. Obligated by custom, though grudging the added burden a little, the Tuliks' relatives helped with the building of a small one-room split log house, and provided a stove made from an empty fuel drum. After four of Sam Tulik's dogs died this winter, from starvation some said, the relatives took him with them to gather wood, to hunt and to fish, until he could beg or buy enough dogs for his own team again.

The Tulik baby, like almost everything that comes their way, seemed doomed from the start. True, the visiting nurse examined Norma Tulik when she was pregnant and found everything all right. She could foresee no complications and therefore did not authorize Norma to fly to the hospital on a government-paid ticket. Norma would have liked to go, but though the hospital is free, the Tuliks did not have forty dollars for the plane ticket. Besides, Norma would have had to go in on the mail plane a week or two before the baby was due, and she had no relatives to stay with in the town until she started labor.

The delivery itself was easy, but the baby breathed with difficulty almost from the beginning. She cried fretfully, nursed lethargically, coughed; then began to run a fever. Concerned, Mr. Elsen radioed the hospital. The doctor prescribed penicillin shots. When the baby was no better by the third evening, the doctor authorized a charter plane to bring mother and child to the hospital.

Next morning Mr. Elsen hurried to check the weather before radioing the charter service. He opened his door to find a heavy snow fog lying on the village; the houses were gone, he could barely see the figure coming toward him up the hill. No matter about the fog, the plane; the figure was Sam Tulik, come to "borrow" a little lumber for a coffin.

In time, with help, the Tuliks may yet succeed, but they look somehow as though they have lost whatever hope and ambition they might once have had. The two Tulik children are unkempt and dirty; they cry easily and often, defenselessly, faces open, arms hanging at their sides, without anger, without expectation.

Norma visits around more than most women in Makumiut; to escape the confines of a house so small there is no room even for a table? A house so small one can tend the stove while sitting on the bed against the opposite wall? Norma is often in her cousin Ruby's house, sitting on the old Gussuk sofa, hands palm up and idle in her lap.

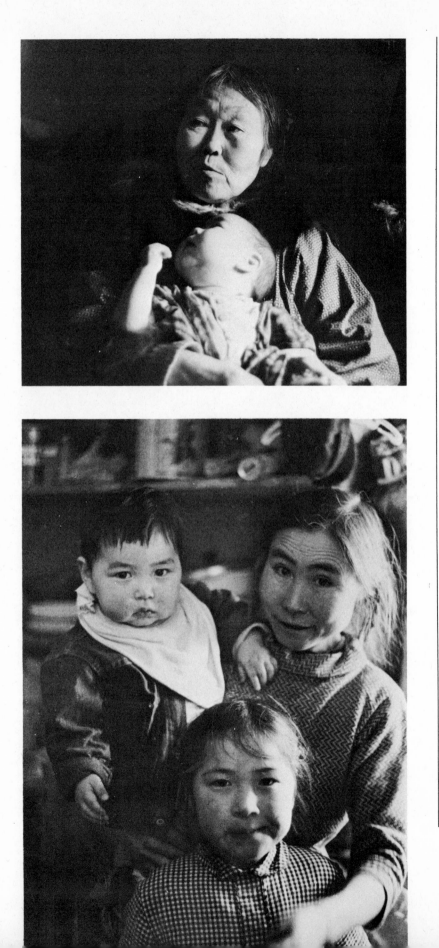

Around the Village

■ Makumiut babies are as housebound in winter as their mothers. Just as they are enveloped in quilts at night in a warm corner of the bed beside their mothers, so they are enveloped all day in the atmosphere of their homes—warm, dark, close—and by the attentions of their families.

Unless their mothers are unusually hard-pressed and there are no older children in the household, babies are bathed, fed, amused, rocked, hugged, carried about, or simply held, for most of their waking hours. They are unhurriedly fed whenever they cry, or given a piece of bread to chew when old enough. They grow fat, and their skin is white and soft, like rising dough. They are passive, content to lie back and watch the passing scene, lacking any great desire to make contact with it. They are seldom allowed to crawl on the floor, and most do not walk until they are well over a year old. When they start, the families delight in encouraging them, and laugh proudly at every attempt. The amount of clothes necessary to keep toddlers warm outside would also immobilize them, and they stay indoors in winter most of the time until they are two years old or more.

The horizons of children widen slowly, evenly. They move from a cocoon of quilts in their houses, surrounded by their families, out into the village, small, safe and familiar. Paradoxically, this environment, where life is more precarious than in American cities and suburbs, is at the same time more understandable and secure for little children.

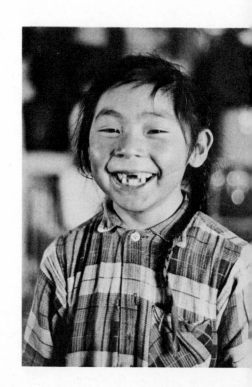

■ Annie Chiftak and her small neighbor want to go out to see the *mukluk* Annie's father is butchering, so her mother bundles her up and goes along.

A crowd has gathered, for this is the biggest of the seals, and its one hundred and fifty pounds of rich dark meat will be eaten by many in the village tonight. Annie's grandmother and her two great-aunts, all of whom she calls by the same kin term, *mahuluk*, are already there. One of the girls watching is Annie's big sister, three of the boys are her brothers, two her uncles. Most of the others are cousins.

Annie wrinkles her nose at the strong smell of warm blood and entrails, for her father has already skinned the seal. Later, her mother will soak the skin in soapy water until the fur has loosened, then scrape and stretch it tightly on a frame to dry. Thick and tough, it will make enough soles for the family's Christmas boots. Father is slicing back the thick layer of pure white fat surrounding the flesh. It will be shared with their relatives, for the clear pale yellow oil is much prized for eating with all food—dried or frozen fish, meat or fowl.

When the stomach cavity is opened, Mother sets Annie down and goes off with the slippery mass of coiled intestines. She quickly runs them through her fingers, squeezing out the food matter and emptying it in a tin of blood saved for the dogs. Slit, washed, and dried, the intestines will be stitched around and around into a raincoat for Father. He still prefers its light weight and wide cut to the plastic and rubber raincoats his sons buy from Sears, even though seal gut must be handled carefully and hung in the cache house where it will neither rot from moisture nor crack from dry heat.

Annie is tired of watching now and turns away. "Come sledding," says her aunt, eight-year-old Gemma.

Most of the children are playing outdoors now. On sheets of cardboard, seal skins, home-made or store-

bought sleds, and even on the backs of their soft fur parkas, they slide down drifts by their houses, or along the winding ravine where the stream gurgles faintly far beneath the snow and ice. The more adventurous climb the hill above the village, almost to the base of *chimuk*, the rock outcropping. From here their world is spread out before them; the village, the tundra, the sky. Running on the hard-packed snow, parka furs streaming in the wind, they flop on their sleds and careen downhill, past the school, the church, between the houses, coming to rest at the very bottom of the village, almost at the snow-covered boats pulled up from the stream.

The View from the School

■ Early in their lives, Makumiut children see the school not just as a building which dominates the village by its site, size, and construction, but also as the center of Gussuk influence. They are taken there when sick for medicines and other treatment, and when well for check-ups, TB tests and inoculations given by the visiting nurse or doctor. The teachers themselves loom large to children, for the Elsens, besides teaching all classes through eighth grade, run radio communication with the outside world, house Gussuk visitors to Makumiut, hold dances for the teen-agers and village meetings and are called upon for advice and help for everything from filling out unemployment compensation forms to giving penicillin shots. A first visit to the teachers' living quarters is astonishing to children— it is like walking straight into the Sears Roebuck catalog. Rugs, upholstered chairs and sofas, ruffled curtains, glowing table lamps, the ceiling pale and high overhead, painted yellow walls far away on all sides; Cinderella's palace could not be more surprising.

But actually starting school marks the big jump into Gussuk life. From the first day a little girl, swamped in her new winter parka, trudges shyly up the hill to the white frame building, her world is enlarged in ways bewildering, frightening, exciting, satisfying, frustrating and enjoyable.

In the early days of Alaskan Eskimo schools, the emphasis was on teaching the three R's and useful manual skills—carpentry, sewing, cooking native foods. The

few schools were staffed by missionaries, trained teachers from Outside, and Eskimos of varying educations. They met in churches, orphanages, log cabins or the teacher's house.

All this is changed now; every village with a population of over a hundred and twenty-five people has an elementary school. Most are run by the federal Bureau of Indian Affairs, though the state of Alaska plans to take them over as it can afford to. Most, like the Makumiut school, are modern, well-equipped, and therefore, in this isolated place, extraordinarily expensive. The cost of schooling per pupil is twice the national average. The program is good standard United States public school fare. Its avowed purpose: "to prepare children for high school." The books and materials are ample, delivered yearly, right down to the Mother Goose rhymes and "art" prints for the walls.

In one room, Mrs. Elsen teaches beginners through fourth grade, thirty children in all. They are sitting at their desks now, one group with "Dick and Jane" readers, others choosing stories from the library shelves, the rest writing in workbooks. Mrs. Elsen has snatched a few minutes to complete some of her school records. She had meant to finish monthly reports yesterday afternoon, but Tom Apureen came up and asked her help in balancing his post office accounts. Then last night Ruby Jim brought her husband to visit for the first time, and Mrs. Elsen didn't want to risk hurting their feelings by saying she was too busy.

She looks up as Catherine Atootuk comes into the room. Catherine, who is new at the job of school cook, has forgotten to soak the kidney beans overnight; now what can she cook for lunch? Regretfully, Mrs. Elsen closes her notebooks and goes out to the storeroom.

Next door, as the older children come in from recess, Mr. Elsen quickly finishes tacking up some of their drawings, shaking his head wryly over Amelia Apureen's. During art period Amelia had started to crayon a "sampler" with "Home Sweet Home" lettered across the middle. Mr. Elsen, who is very tired of samplers, suggested she make something she had seen. Dutifully, she set it aside and started on the stereotypic American children's house, with four windows, a door, and on either side, a row of stiff-stalked flowers in front of a picket fence. Mr. Elsen then suggested she make *her* house. After some thought, Amelia selected a white crayon, carefully drew a white line across her paper, and above it, a round, white, snow-block "igloo."

Now it's social studies time, and the sixth grade is starting to read about a printshop in colonial America. The children can read the words quite competently, but the meaning? Printing press? *Colonial* America? England? Mr. Elsen sits down with them to talk about it. Where to begin? The gulf between this material and their real knowledge seems unbridgeable. He tries to start a discussion; Hiram Chiftak says simply, "Gussuks make everything."

The next group is struggling through a chapter on the potato industry in northern Maine, and there are only ten minutes left for this lesson. As Mr. Elsen calls them together, he wonders if they've ever even *seen* a potato; he wishes he had some left from the crate he got on the *North Star*.

Meanwhile, the sixth graders help each other with the test at the end of their lesson, so that none of them should either fail or be outstanding; then they go on, promptly at eleven-thirty, to spelling.

What happens to children who are surrounded by this mass of information, much of which is foreign to their culture, half-understood, grasped too poorly to allow for satisfying use, and who must express themselves in a second language that further constricts them? Part of the answer is that they have the saving power to simply turn off much that is meaningless or confusing. What they can really grasp they take pleasure in; the excitement of finding a story in a mass of squiggly lines, the satisfaction of writing a nice flowing script, the mental exercise of being able to manipulate numbers with increasing skill. Much of their schooling, of course, will be of use in their adult lives; it may be vital if they try to leave Makumiut and settle Outside. But Amelia's "house" and snow igloo are nevertheless symbols of the separation from her world that the school cannot help but promote.

Two Worlds

■ Young people in Makumiut have the same struggles as their contemporaries everywhere: to find out who they are, what their relationship with the opposite sex is or should be, what they want to become. In addition, they bear the burden of being between two vastly different ways of life. Often resentful of one or the other, completely comfortable in neither, they must nevertheless live with both.

The view from school of Gussuk life with its abundance of goods and its nice clean children moving confidently and successfully through the amazing world of cities, highways, factories and stores—this view inevitably adds to the other Gussuk influences that make the young people feel backward and inadequate. It is indeed ironic that the attempt to bring education, material comforts and medical care to an isolated Eskimo village should result in a higher standard of living and a lower standard of personal worth. In Makumiut, this, even more than the crowded houses, the lack of toilets and running water, or the low cash incomes, is poverty. And it is the young people here who are hardest hit; they live with the white man's "culture of poverty" and with the poverty of their own culture.

Most teen-agers have not gone on to boarding school for secondary education. They do not see the use of it, or their families cannot meet even the small fees involved, or they are needed to help out at home, or they simply don't want to go so far away. Of those who have attended boarding school, most have returned to Makumiut, to the few jobs requiring western education, or to hunting and fishing, housekeeping and baby-tending.

One young couple "relocated" Outside with Bureau of Indian Afairs help, but came back within a year; they were unhappy in California. One young man has turned a traditional craft to modern profit *in* Makumiut. A skilful and talented ivory carver, he sells immediately everything he makes.

And of the others:

■ Louise Angiak likes to go up the hill and visit the teachers in the winter evenings. While Mrs. Elsen mends, makes out reports, or does her baking, Louise drinks endless cups of tea, or sits, hands folded across her stomach, fingers picking idly at her nail polish. She talks quietly, in a slow monotonous sing-song, her voice lost occasionally beneath the sound of the wind whistling down the hill, pushing around the house.

"Gee, I had a real good time in Anchorage. I mean, we went dancing, and to the movies, and Bob, that's my boyfriend, he's in the Air Force, he's an Airman 1st Class, he likes to buy me all these things, like earrings, and scarfs . . . you know, he gave me this sweater I got on. He's real cute, even he's kind of fat. As soon as he's got enough money, he's going to send me a ticket to Anchorage . . .

"I kind of wish I didn't come back here, but they kept writing me my mom was too lonesome, and she's getting real old, and well, there was this Mrs. Donaldson, she kept coming to see me about a BIA authorization ticket for me to come back here. I was supposed to come as soon as I got out of the hospital, but I didn't want to then . . . I got a real good job in the Air Force canteen, that's where I met Bob, my boyfriend . . . well, then I got fired from that job, there was this mean guy who ran the kitchen, he said I kept coming to work late . . . and well, Bob said maybe I should go back and see my mom, and as soon as he had the money he'd send me a ticket to Anchorage . . . the Air Force sends a lot of his pay to his wife in Georgia or California or somewhere, but he's going to get a divorce, he wants to marry me . . .

"You know, I really like the way you fixed up this room, those little plates on the wall, they're cute. Mrs. Bingham, they were our last teachers, she had it fixed up just nice, too. I was going to fix up our house, I was making some curtains, but our sewing machine's bum, I don't know what it is . . .

"Gee, I hope my boyfriend sends me that ticket soon, I really like it in Anchorage."

■ When he was a young man, Jeremiah was baptized by the itinerant Catholic priest. Then a census taker came along, saying Jeremiah should have two names, so he gave as the second one Snahkamiu, which means simply "coast dweller." He didn't consider using any of his Eskimo names, for it was taboo to refer to oneself by name.

When Jeremiah Snahkamiu's son was born sixteen years ago, Jeremiah called him Chuskuk. For the priest he fumbled with Gussuk names, and thought of Jimmy Jeremiah, dropping Snahkamiu entirely.

During Jimmy's last year at Makumiut school, some boys translated his Eskimo name into English, literally "cup." It had never sounded foolish in Eskimo—everyone knew it was an old, old name in the village—but in English it was a big joke. They called him Empty Cup, Dirty Cup, Coffee Cup, Tea Cup. The next year he went off to boarding school and there he realized that the name Jimmy Jeremiah wasn't even considered a regular Gussuk name.

Last summer, when he came home from vacation, he said he didn't want to return to school, he was tired of being "bossed around." His parents neither questioned him nor tried to change his mind—it would have been inquisitive and directive.

85

Fall came and Jimmy, an incompetent and uninterested fisherman and hunter, spent more and more time hanging about Mike David's store cadging cigarettes when he could and strumming tunelessly on a battered guitar.

A couple of months ago he began to stay all day in his house, a single small room, emerging only at night to lean against the outside wall of the store and watch the teen-agers fooling around in the light. Then he stopped coming out at all, and rumors began to circulate quietly around the village.

Grandmother Chahnak, who is Jeremiah's sister, said Jimmy was going wild in there, busting things up— why, he had broken the leg off the stove. She was sure he was bewitched, she had seen it before. Then Jimmy's parents moved out of the house, taking shelter with their nephew, Matthew Fisher. This was traditional Makumiut treatment of a disturbed person—after all, *they* were capable of rational behavior, while he obviously was not. And of course a main consideration was avoiding a commotion. Jeremiah remembered stories of a whole small community which had once packed up and left a madman.

Late one night in the following week, Jimmy burst into the Fishers' house, threatening, in English, to kill his parents. They struggled up from the floor where they were sleeping, moving back against the wall. Matthew managed to steer Jimmy out the door, calm him down and send him home to bed.

The next morning, Jeremiah's brother, whose house is nearest Jimmy's, suddenly decided he needed to visit a relative in Salmon Creek. He hurriedly packed his wife and children into his sled and left. Jeremiah and Matthew went to talk to Mr. Elsen, who got on the radio and received authorization to send Jimmy in to the hospital on the next mail plane.

When the plane arrived on Monday, Mr. Elsen had to get Jimmy; Jeremiah and Matthew had both gone needlefishing. He found Jimmy surprisingly agreeable to the idea of going to the hospital. The doctor reported on the radio next day that he was behaving perfectly normally, and on the following Monday he came back to Makumiut. Tuesday he burst into the Fishers' house and threatened his parents again.

Next day Jeremiah and Matthew again went to the school, sending a telegram for the state trooper to come and take Jimmy away.

Now everyone is waiting for the trooper to arrive. Jimmy's neighbors stay indoors at night as much as possible and avoid his house by day. When the trooper comes, a Village Council meeting will be held and charges made. The trooper will escort Jimmy, looking composed if surly, down to the plane, while from inside their houses people watch them go by. Then everyone will try to forget the whole business, and they will not mention Jimmy again.

Jeremiah's brother will bring his family home from Salmon Creek and settle in again. Jeremiah and his wife will move back into their house, propping the stove up on an old fuel tin.

■ Ever since Christina came back from River Village, fifty miles inland from Makumiut, she has seemed surrounded by an atmosphere secret, quiet, contented, and yet flurried with excitement. Even her father notices it, though he says nothing. Her mother wonders what happened at River Village, but it has nothing to do with that.

Christina went there when her newly married sister wrote that she was lonesome, and Christina soon saw why. She thought the little village much too old-time. Her brother-in-law's family objected every time her sister washed his clothes in the same tub with hers, an old taboo she had only vaguely heard of. They criticized the girl's cooking, saying it was too Gussuk, and when Christina went out to chop firewood on the day after the old grandfather died, she was scolded so badly for this breach of custom that she resolved to go home at the first chance. She was sorry to leave her sister, but it was too bum there. Anyway, she hoped her brother-in-law could eventually be persuaded to come and settle in Makumiut.

Lots of boys in River Village had been after her, for she was the liveliest girl there, but they only made her think the more of Daniel. This was the other reason she had wanted to come back so soon.

Now, Christina spends hours daydreaming, washing her straight black hair, putting it up in pink rollers and brushing it out as she sits by the window. She giggles often, warmly, involuntarily, at any provocation, or at none. Almost every afternoon she watches Daniel's sled returning home across the tundra. She recognizes him first by his father's team, which has a small leader, and then by the big white wolf ruff of the new jacket he always wears. She is proud of him, for he is already a skilful hunter and fisherman.

She meets him almost every evening outside Edward Chahnak's brightly lit store where the teen-agers gather. Last fall he used to tease her and chase her out into the dark, snow-glowing night, but now they more often stand near the corner of the building, talking quietly from time to time. She is aware, without conscious thought, of the way he stands, shoulders hunched, hands deep in his narrow jeans pockets, moving lightly about to keep warm. She notes with amusement the faint frost which forms, as he talks, on the sparse hairs of his upper lip. This summer, he says, he wants to build a house for them, using split logs of driftwood. If he can earn enough money at fish camp, he can buy glass windows and a stove for it. She listens, answers vaguely, giggles, slips her arms inside her parka and across her warm chest.

A few times they have slipped off to his father's cache house to be alone, but Christina doesn't much like it.

It is cold there and she is afraid of the mice she knows are around, but she wonders what it would be like to live in the same house alone with him.

■ With a dozen other young men, Mike David went to Anchorage a few weeks ago for yearly National Guard duty. He found Anchorage gratingly noisy, crowded, baffling and belittling of himself. One night he picked up a prostitute who turned out to his disgust to be an Indian, and then was worried he'd get "that sickness."

He came back yesterday with a cold, an eighty-cent loaf of store bread, two grapefruit, a fifth of whiskey, and the nagging memory of a tourist in a bar who had stared at him with such evident curiosity, that Mike, fortified by a few beers, surprised himself by leaning into the man's face and saying, "Want to take a picture?"

He was equally surprised to find that Makumiut on his return looked to him small, dirty and dull. He shared the whiskey last night with his cousin Eddie, the two of them taking hurried gulps in the back room of his house, until Mike remembered that Eddie had borrowed an old ice pick from him last year and had never returned it. Eddie insisted he had returned it, and that anyway it had originally belonged to *his* father, though in fact he had broken it and had never wanted to tell Mike. Eddie drew himself uncertainly up and called Mike a "basserd liar." Mike tried to sock him, lost his balance and hit his hand on the doorway. Eddie passed out in the cold night beside a cache house, where his father luckily found him and pulled him home.

This morning, with the whiskey gone, Mike wanted to start a pot of homebrew. Going through his wife's food cupboard, looking for yeast, he remembered the evening's happenings and grew more embarrassed and more angry. When he had fallen by mistake on the baby, asleep in their bed, his wife had scolded him in front of Eddie, bundled up the baby and run off to her mother's house. She had not yet returned, the house was cold, and the only breakfast he had had was one hard sourdough roll, the last in the box. Trying to reach the yeast packages that his wife had hidden, he had just knocked over the sugar jar when he heard the faint whine of the mail plane coming over the hills.

As manager of the Village Cooperative Native Store, he had to hurry over to the post office for the goods that should arrive that week. Eddie helped him carry back to the store the boxes of snowmobile parts, the frozen haunches of reindeer meat from Nunivak Island, and the bundles of rabbit skins from Seattle. In the course of working together, the night's quarrel was covered over, at least until the next pot of homebrew could be started. And Mike was far too busy selling goods and settling the complicated accounts arising from payment by government check, cash, furs and mail order house refund slips to think of starting a pot himself.

By evening, the store has taken in a hundred and fifty dollars, and Mike is filling out an order for nylon fishnet, which the cooperative can now afford to buy in bulk at wholesale price. He is pleased with himself, for the store has prospered under his direction; he keeps clear books, places orders promptly, and has nearly repaid the Bureau of Indian Affairs loan. True, he is not as skilful a hunter as his contemporaries—he was away at boarding school for too many years—but his job is a respected one in the community.

Lucy, Mike's wife, returned home earlier this evening when he sent his little brother over to say there was a big piece of reindeer meat for her. She stands by the stove now, stirring the boiling pot, the baby warm and almost asleep on her hip. Stepping over to the bed, she gently rolls him in a quilt and returns to the stove to ladle out two steaming bowls of meat and broth. As she comes toward the table, Mike finishes his order and looks up, smiling tentatively at her.

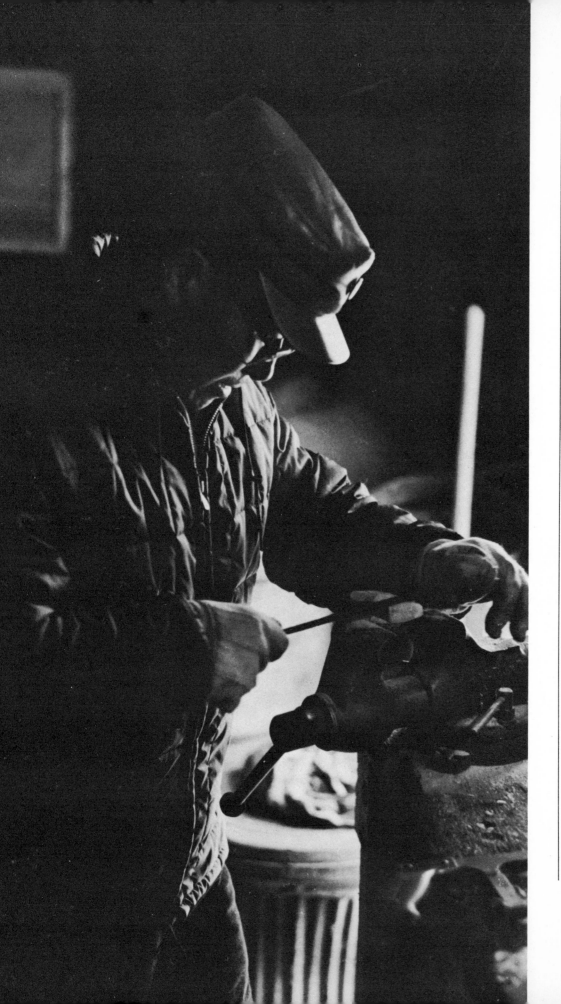

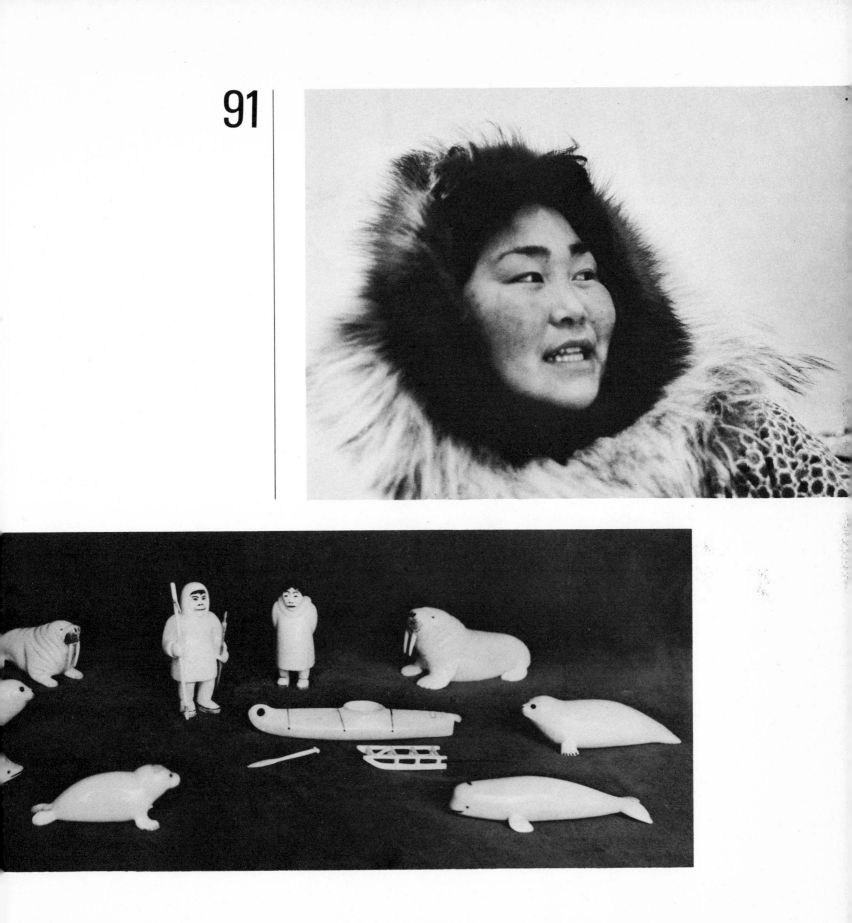

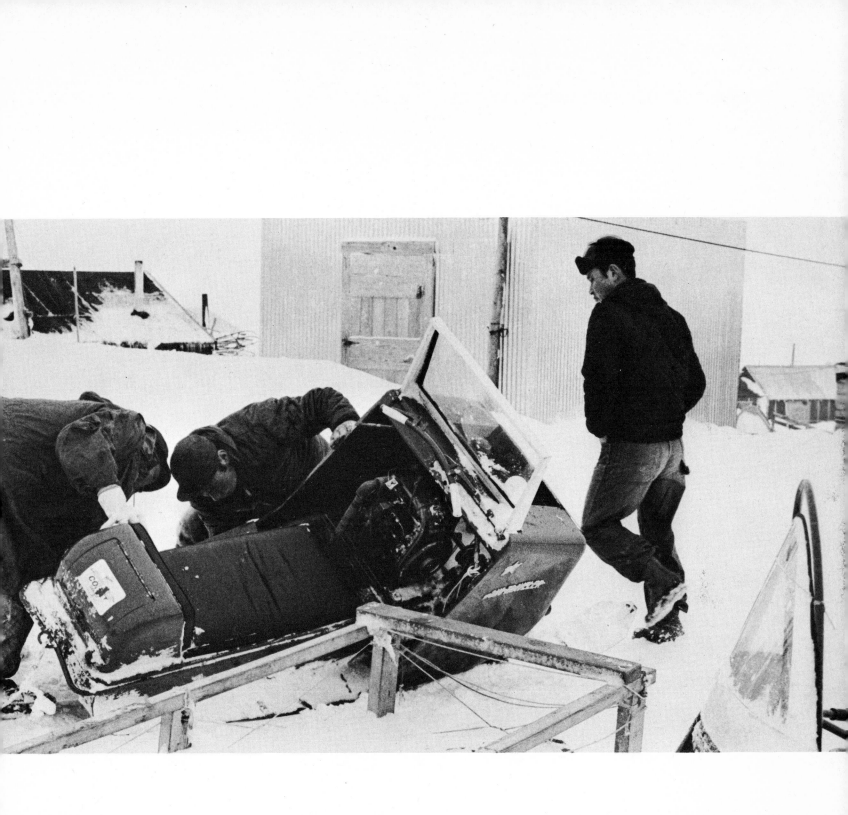

The Trail

■ A common notion of modern man is that his ancestors stand behind him, he faces the future, he explores new frontiers. But in Makumiut there is traditionally a different view. A young man in his twenties, who is well aware of the great technological changes now taking place—the increasing use of steel tools, of nylon nets, metal traps, of outboard motors and snowmobiles —says this: "Our ancestors are in front of us. We follow in the trail of our ancestors. We use the same methods of food capture. There is nothing new. Things go on."

And it is true that, even with contemporary technology, a Makumiut man must use each day the detailed knowledge and skills of his forefathers, for the ages-old web of animal life in the Arctic is delicate, subject to extreme pressures of many kinds. Most of the hunted birds, fish and mammals are transient, each species spending only part of the year within reach of Makumiut people. Even in the area, both the movements and abundance of game vary radically, often unpredictably, from year to year, from month to month. In addition, the effects of tide, current and weather cause major changes from day to day. In winter, the riches of the land are almost all out of sight, moving in intricate patterns beneath the cover of snow and ice. Except when shooting foxes, seals, or ptarmigan, the

In winter, the riches of the land
are almost out of sight

hunter is literally on one plane, the hunted are hidden several feet below him.

Thus the daily search for food, clothing or fuel involves weighing and balancing many factors. A man must decide what is available, what he most needs, where it can be found, and how he can reach it. He considers the weather, both present and expected, for weather changes often and with subtle warning. Fog or snowfall may cut visibility to three feet in a matter of minutes; a dangerous time to be caught out hunting on the sea. The direction and force of the wind must be taken into account. A wind from the south will produce great turbulence on the tundra to the north of the hills but a pocket of calm on the windward slopes—a good time to go over there to check a fish trap. If a wind is very strong, it can make a storm from snow already fallen, a storm so strong and so prolonged that, though one can faintly glimpse blue sky overhead, ground travel is all but impossible for several days.

A man always carefully considers the condition of the trail, for he does not travel freely over the face of the land. Though it looks vast and undifferentiated to the outsider, the Makumiut man sees it as structured in its own way as a system of roads and highways is to a motorist. Does he want to go over the hills? There is one low pass that has determined the trail there. Is that trail covered by new snow that will slow him down, or is it hard-packed and smooth so that he can be home again by dark? Has it been affected by a warm wind or by high tides which cause the streams at the base of the hills to overflow? If so, his dogs' feet may become wet, then ice-encrusted, cut and bleeding.

Last of all a man considers where others are going—for safety, for cooperation, for company.

In the old days, families followed a pattern of shifting settlement adapted to the seasonal movements of fish and mammals, and to Eskimo custom. Josiah Chiftak remembers all of this. In summer his family, with others, traveled north along the coast to fish the salmon run and put up a temporary shelter of sod, snow, skins, driftwood and sedge mat. In fall they moved to a permanent semisubterranean house of driftwood and sod on the inland tundra. There they fished the blackfish and whitefish concentrations and trapped fur-bearing animals. In winter they rejoined the other families in Makumiut and began a series of ceremonial events and exchange of visits with other communities which lasted throughout the darkest time of the year.

All of these seasonal camps were damp, cold and dark. With few metal tools, little wood could be gathered for burning. There was never enough seal oil to use for heating the houses. Most fish and meat was eaten raw, much still partially frozen. Fires were made in houses only when the layer of ice inside became unbearably thick. In Makumiut itself, Josiah lived in the *kazigi*, the men's house. There he learned all the traditions and religious beliefs of his people. There dances were rehearsed and held, and there each evening old stories were told until he dropped off to sleep on the row of platforms lining the driftwood walls of the house.

With the advent of the first Russian traders, this pattern began to change. The traders offered guns, ammunition, canvas tents, iron tools, needles, matches, in exchange for furs. People began to trap more and to gather at these trading posts. By the time the Americans had taken over Alaska, the trading post meant a stable source of food and gear.

Using steel ice picks and fine mesh cotton nets, a man could catch enough needlefish to feed a team of seven dogs. And with a seven dog team, he could forage over a far larger area. Thus it was feasible for him to stay in his winter village much of the year. And the village grew in size, since the larger foraging area could support a larger number of people.

Today only the old fall camps are still in use, and many of these are being abandoned. Scattered miles apart across the inland tundra, each was the center of a trapping area. Tiny, half-underground, they were the dwelling places of whole extended families. Now they are occupied only by the men—brothers, fathers and sons, cousins—who go out for a few days or a week at a time, to set spring traps on the tundra for red and white foxes, basket traps in the streams for mink, otter and muskrat.

Trapping is one of the few chances a man has to earn cash for the Gussuk goods which are increasingly desired and depended upon. If the season is poor, or if fur fashions Outside suddenly change, he may find his

efforts nearly wasted. But in an average season, he will make several hundred dollars from the sale of furs, and his wife will have many muskrat skins for the family's own parkas.

By January the ice in the streams is too thick for underwater traps to be feasible, and the men return permanently, with evident pleasure, to the comforts of the village.

In winter, as in summer, fish are the most important source of food.

The freshwater fish, which have been dispersed during the open season, feeding and growing in the vast inland area of shallow ponds, are forced by the increasing thickness of ice in fall to concentrate in deeper, continuously flowing streams. They remain sealed under the ice, in the dark, in the muddy gray water, throughout the winter. There is little food there and great cold; the fish are sluggish, move slowly, grow thinner. Each kind of fish has a different pattern of movement. The Makumiut men know and follow all of these, hidden from sight though they are, and catch them with almost as many devices as there are species of fish.

In volume and number, the tiny needlefish, used for dog food, form the greatest part of the winter catch. Abandoning the frozen ponds, they gather in tundra creeks in immense schools, sometimes over a mile in length, drifting back and forth with the tide, moving every few days into a new area.

With a dog team requiring two hundred pounds of needlefish a week, it is necessary to follow these schools constantly. When one has been located, the men can predict its probable movements by their knowledge of the tides and of the order prevailing in a school of fish, the larger ones being consistently downstream of the smaller.

Every morning, several men will head their teams out across the tundra to the preferred creeks. If the same place has been used the previous day, they have only to chip loose and scoop out the ice which has accumulated over the holes during the night. But if they must choose a new place, a slot four feet by a foot and a half must be chopped, sometimes through as much as four feet of ice. Occasionally, the men will find they have miscalculated and have lost the school. Without complaint or annoyance, they move on to try another spot, helping each other with the chipping, at last thrusting their nets through the open slots, down to the bottom of the creek, and turning them to face the current.

It is necessary to follow the schools of needlefish constantly

Simon Angiak is hauling his net up; the sack heaves with fish, a wriggling mass that begins to freeze almost as soon as it is lifted into the air. He empties it onto the ice and quickly replaces the net in its hole before the meshes freeze stiff and heavy.

The men work easily at this, smoothly, moving around to keep warm. They talk quietly to each other from time to time, raising their voices only to shout at an occasional pair of growling dogs. The wind whistles across the snow. The creek ice cracks loudly, regularly, along the banks, as the whole surface is raised or lowered by the tide. At midday a couple of camp stoves are taken out of the sleds, snow is melted in coffee pots, tea made, and dried or frozen fish eaten. By midafternoon the sky is darkening; when the first person begins to pack up, the others follow suit, and in a matter of minutes the teams are racing each other home across the tundra, each sled with its one to two hundred pound load of fish.

The tomcod swim all the way out to sea in winter, running down the river in such numbers for a few weeks that they are scooped up in nets or, more commonly, hooked on unbaited lines decorated with bits of shiny metal and red felt. This is a favorite activity of girls and boys in after-school hours. They sit or squat on the river ice, like Andrew Fisher, watching intently the small circle of muddy water. When the shadowy gray shapes appear, swirling about the line, nudging the old pieces of tin can, he jerks his stick swiftly up. Another fish lands on the ice, turning white and rigid even as he looks at it.

Later in the winter, lush fish move from tundra creeks to spawn in the freshwater streams along the hills. The tall handsome split driftwood traps are still used to catch them, but are being superseded by more easily made ones of chicken wire. For these traps, stick

*Unbaited lines, nets,
and driftwood traps are
used to catch fish*

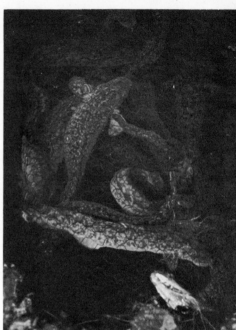

Sometimes chicken wire traps are pushed through long trenches to catch fish

fences are made and pushed through long trenches chopped in the ice. Stuck firmly into the muddy bottom, they serve to direct the fish into the trap. Lush are prized at this time for their rich eggs and large liver, a welcome change of flavor.

By late winter the supply of dried salmon and herring is long gone, and available fresh fish are lean and watery. The people begin to look forward to spring sealing and to hope that it may be a good season.

When the clouds over the sea reflect the dark gray of open water, men head downriver by dog team, camp on the bay shores, and move out across the sea ice. With the help of the "sky map" they seek the flaw—the edge of the land-fast ice—and the leads of open water stretching out between the sheets of pack ice. Here traditional gear is still the best to use, though with some modifications. The beautifully made, light driftwood kayak is now covered with canvas instead of the harder-to-maintain sealskin. The hunter leaves his dog team or snowmobile and walks, pulling his kayak on its own small sled. At a lead, he puts the kayak in the water, loads the sled onto the back of it, and paddles off, watching for swimming seals. If the lead ends in pack ice, he simply reverses the procedure, walking, pulling the sled, until he comes to another lead.

It is not surprising that a few magic rituals are still associated with sealing, for it can be dangerous. On a bitterly cold day, ice may form on the open water and cut the kayak. Even more hazardous, a strong off-shore wind may blow masses of pack ice away from the flaw, taking the hunter willy-nilly with it. Josiah Chiftak still tells of the time in his youth that he spent several days on a floating ice cake, and when at last he reached shore again, feared he would lose his hands and feet from frostbite.

Some years seals are practically inaccessible. With

112

*The need for firewood
is unending*

*Traditional gear is still
used for sealing*

very low temperatures the layer of land-fast ice extends far out to sea, and unfavorable winds may close the distant leads. Then the seals are farther away than Makumiut men venture, for these people are more chary of the sea than many Eskimo groups.

But the rewards of sealing are many: skins for clothing, fresh meat for food, and much oil, for at this time seals have a thick layer of fat to keep them warm during the winter.

Less interesting, but no less necessary, is the unending need for firewood. Caches of summer's driftwood are sufficient only to supplement the use of willow and alder bushes. It seems surprising that the scrubby growth along the base of the hills can still provide enough wood, year after year, to keep most of the houses in Makumiut warm all winter long. But every day, if the weather permits, several of the men go out and chop a sledful each in a few hours.

Unless the weather is too bad, Makumiut men feel it their place to "go out" each day. Even Josiah Chiftak, in his seventies, is loath to stay around the village. He feels his wife will think the less of him; he will himself. Even he prepares each morning for an "engagement with the environment."

Makumiut men face the uncertainty, unpredictability, danger and frustration of their world straight-forwardly, patiently, with knowledge and calm. Out on the tundra and sea they feel inferior to no one, resentful of no one, confronted by few problems of human relations. They are, without thinking about it, in touch with their environment and able to survive in this most rigorous of worlds by a long process of adaptation and ingenuity—the trail of their ancestors.

Then, at the close of each day, the thin black lines turn back again across the vast landscape, converging on the place where

There is a village,
set on a hill
beside a river,
where the river enters the sea...